THE
APACHES

AND PUEBLO PEOPLES OF THE SOUTHWEST

ALYS SWAN-JACKSON

Heinemann

Acknowledgements

The publishers would like to thank Richard Green, and Richard Cupidi of the Public House Bookshop, Brighton, for their assistance; Bill Donohoe of Sharpline Studios and Jonathan Adams, who illustrated the see-through scenes; James Field, who illustrated the cover; and the organizations that have given their permission to reproduce the following pictures:

AA&AC: 6 top left, 12 top right. **American Philosophical Society:** 35 top left.
Arizona State Museum: 12 top left, 23 top right, /Helga Teiwes 7 bottom right.
Bridgeman Art Library: 30 top left. **British Museum/M Holford/Reed:** 38 top left.
C. M. Dixon: 4 top left, 4 bottom centre, 28 top left, 36 top left. **Denver Art Museum/Reed:** 11 bottom.
Denver Public Library/Reed: 13 bottom left. **Museum of American Indian/Reed:** 31 top right.
Museum of Mankind: 26 top right, 27 bottom left, 32 bottom left. **Museum of Northern Arizona:** 32 top left, /Marc Gaede 19 bottom right. **North Wind Pictures:** 14 top left, 22 bottom left 36 top right, 36 centre right, 39 top right, 43 bottom right. **Peter Newark's American Pictures:** 4 bottom left, 19 bottom right.
ProFiles West/John A. Sawyer: 6 top right, 45 top right, /Wiley/Wales 17, /Jack Hoehn, Jr 44 top right, /P. Barry Levy 45 top left. **Richard Green Collection/Brian Walkenden:** 18 bottom left, 27 bottom right, 31 top left.
Robert Harding Picture Library/Walter Rawlings: 26 top left, /Adam Woolfit 38 top right.
Smithsonian Institution National Anthropological Archives: 15 top left.
Smithsonian Institution/John Freeman/Reed: 37 bottom right.
University of Regina: 30 top right. **Werner Forman/Arizona State Museum**: 20 top left, /Maxwell Museum of Anthropology, Albuquerque 5 bottom left, /Museum of Northern Arizona 32 top right, /Peabody Museum, Harvard University 4 bottom left, /Schindler Collection, New York 18 top left, 30 centre right.

Illustrators:
Jonathan Adams: 8-9, heading icons. **Richard Berridge:** 30-31. **Bill Donohoe:** 16-17, 24-25, 40-41.
James Field: front cover. **Terry Gabbey (Eva Morris):** 18-19 main picture, 22, 23, 28, 29, 38-39 main picture.
Andre Hrydziuszko: 46-47. **Kevin Madison:** 5 and inset. **Mark Stacey:** 10-11, 14, 15, 20-21 main picture,
21 top right, 34, 35, 42, 43. **Simon Williams:** 6, 7, 12, 19, 26, 27, 32-33 main picture, 36.
Gerald Wood: 13, 20 top right, 24, 28, 29 top right, 37 top left, 44, 45.

In memory of my husband, Robert Joseph Jackson 1945-1990.

Editor: Andrew Farrow
Designer: Nick Avery
Picture researcher: Anna Smith
Production controller: David Lawrence

Other titles in the series:
*The Aztecs, Ancient Rome, Ancient Greece, Ancient Egypt, The Middle Ages,
The Renaissance, The Vikings, The Age of Industry, Forts & Castles,
Tombs & Treasure, The Celts, Plains Indians, Houses & Homes,
Submarines & Ships, The Incas*

First published in Great Britain 1996
by Heinemann Children's Reference,
Halley Court, Jordan Hill, Oxford, OX2 8EJ,
a division of Reed Educational & Professional Publishing Ltd.

MADRID ATHENS PARIS
FLORENCE PORTSMOUTH NH CHICAGO
SAO PAULO SINGAPORE TOKYO
MELBOURNE AUCKLAND IBADAN
GABORONE JOHANNESBURG KAMPALA NAIROBI

ISBN 0 600 58488 7

A CIP catalogue record for this book is available at the British Library.

See Through pages printed by SMIC, France.
Books printed and bound by Proost, Belgium.

CONTENTS

THE SOUTHWEST

Native Americans in the Southwest have been making baskets since prehistoric times. Many fine examples have been found on sites once inhabited by the ancient Anasazi peoples who have consequently become known as the 'Basketmakers'. The Apache learned the skill of basketmaking from these early peoples and have become famous for baskets like this one.

Some early Pueblo communities built homes in the recesses of cliffs. This is Montezuma Castle, in Arizona. It has five storeys and 20 rooms. It accommodated about 15 to 20 families.

The Southwestern area of the United States has been the centre of a number of rich and unique Indian cultures since the first people arrived about 15,000 years ago. Large numbers of American Indian peoples, such as the Pueblo, can still be found in the region, despite the recent domination of the white man. There they live together in clans or tribes, maintaining their traditional way of life.

THE LAND
Even though several rivers – including the Rio Grande, Colorado, Gila and Salt – run through this region, the lands of the Southwest are generally dry. In the north, around the Great Basin, is a high plateau region of steep-walled canyons and plateaux, called mesas, and sandy areas. To the south is flat, desert country. Water is often scarce and drought a real threat.

THE PEOPLES
The best known of the original peoples are the Anasazi, the Mogollon and the Hohokam, who all lived in permanent settlements and farmed the land. They were followed in about AD 1300 by the

'We have lived upon this land from days beyond history's records, far past any living memory, deep into the time of legend. The story of my people and the story of this place are one single story. No man can think of us without thinking of this place. We are always joined together.'

— Pueblo man —

Pueblo tribes of today, who also built villages, and by the Papago, Pima and Yuma, who lived in villages but moved from place to place with the changing seasons. More recently, other hunting and gathering tribes moved about in small bands in search of food. The Apache and Navajo were nomadic peoples who often raided the Pueblos for food and goods.

Mogollon pottery was predominantly plain brown at first, then red-on-brown. Shown below left and right are some 10th century black-and-white painted burial ware called Mimbres. This was broken when its owner died, to symbolically release the soul, and the pieces were placed in the grave. In the centre is a more recent pot from Zuni pueblo.

STRANGERS

Life in the Southwest was transformed by contact with Europeans, who arrived in the Americas in increasing numbers from the 16th century. During the 200 years that followed Columbus' voyages, the Spaniards conquered many of the Indian peoples in South and Central America. Then, in the course of the 19th century, the Indians met a new people.

WHITE AMERICANS

The newcomers were white Americans who had first settled on the east coast of North America 300 years before and were now spreading westwards. Many Indians had to fight for their land. Their whole way of life was threatened by the new settlers. However, despite hardships, some Indian groups have managed to survive and prosper.

This map shows some of the Southwestern peoples mentioned in this book. Their lands cover the present-day states of New Mexico, Arizona, southern Utah, southwest Colorado and part of western Texas.

MOGOLLON = *ancient peoples*
NAVAJO = *tribes today*

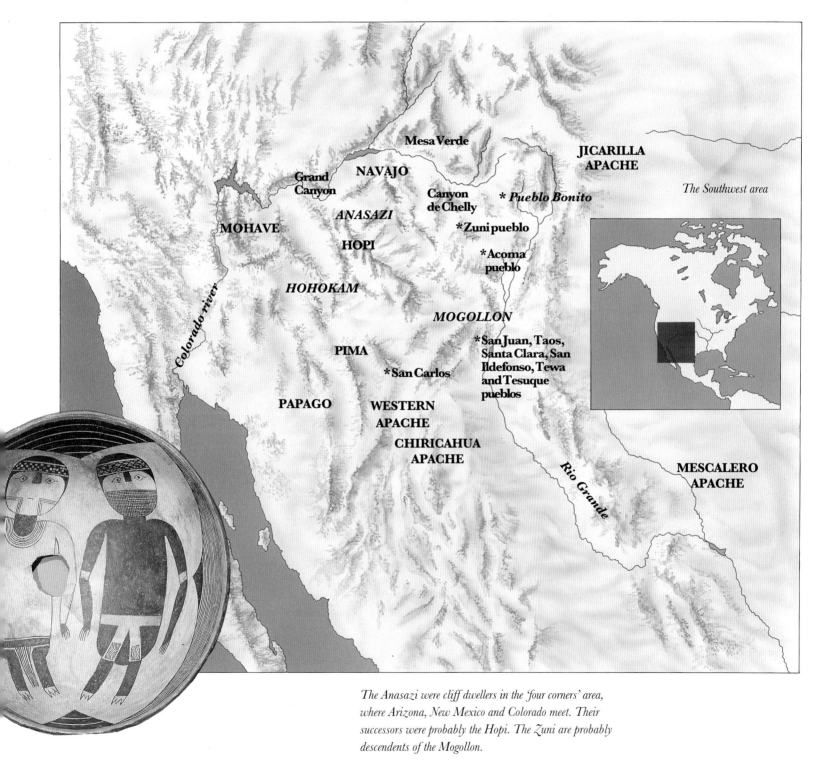

The Southwest area

The Anasazi were cliff dwellers in the 'four corners' area, where Arizona, New Mexico and Colorado meet. Their successors were probably the Hopi. The Zuni are probably descendents of the Mogollon.

EARLY CIVILIZATIONS

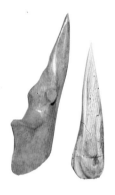

Archaeological remains, such as these bone awls, help us to date the ancient civilizations of the Southwest.

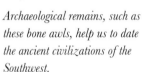

The Paleo-Indians were nomadic groups who hunted mastodons and other big game animals, like this bison, across much of the Southwest during the Ice Age.

The very first people to live in the Americas came from Asia. Some **50,000** years ago, they travelled in groups across the land bridge which then joined Asia to Alaska. Over thousands of years, these people spread slowly southwards through North, Central and South America.

THE DESERT PEOPLE

The earliest human inhabitants of the area were the Paleo-Indians of the late Ice Age, about 10-15,000 years ago. We know from the many stone spear points that have been discovered that they were skilled hunters. They lived off now-extinct species of bison and other game that roamed the region.

Around 9,000 years ago, the weather began to get warmer and dryer, and the people had to adapt to more desert-like conditions. With far fewer large animals to hunt, they began to rely on collecting wild foods, such as pinon pine nuts and various berries, and on trapping small animals.

Petroglyphs are a form of picture writing carved on rocks and cliffs. The decorated rock often marks a sacred site that tells the history of the early Indian peoples.

These desert people, as they were called, sheltered in caves or under over-hanging rocks. They made blankets from rabbit fur and animal hides and tools and utensils from chipped stone, wood and bone.

FARMERS

Next came the early farming cultures, including that of the Hohokam people in central Arizona, the Mogollon of the mountains and deserts of New Mexico, and the Anasazi. The Hohokam were farmers and lived in small villages. (The name Hohokam comes from a Pima Indian word meaning 'those who have gone'.) They built irrigation canals to water their fields of corn and other crops. Weaving, pottery and shell jewellery were important Hohokam crafts.

EARLY HOUSES

The early Hohokam lived in simple houses, each consisting of a round pit covered with a roof of brushwood and layers of soil. As the population increased, however, thick-walled 'adobe' houses with several storeys became more common.

A team of Hohokam workers dig a canal that will bring water from the mountains to irrigate the fields.

MOGOLLON

The Mogollon people are believed to be descended directly from the desert people. Although they are best known as farmers, growing corn and beans, they also hunted bison and other game. The Mogollon built small villages at altitudes above 1,200m. At first these consisted mainly of pit houses, although stone was later used more widely. Mogollon culture is particularly famous for its stonework and its pottery.

ANASAZI

The Anasazi – from a Navajo word meaning 'The Ancient Ones' – were one of the most highly developed civilizations in North America. They lived first in pit houses similar to the Hohokam, growing corn and hunting animals for food. About a thousand years ago, they began to build houses of stone, both in open country and also in caves in the walls of canyons. Some, such as those of the Mesa Verde, Arizona, were like large houses (see pages 8-9). Others, such as those of Chaco Canyon, were huge structures resembling blocks of flats. People climbed ladders to reach their houses, sometimes from the roofs of lower houses to the doors of higher ones.

THE CLIFF DWELLERS

The Anasazi built their stone cities and lived in them for 200-300 years. Then something happened, and the stone cities were mysteriously abandoned. It may have been that a 20-year drought, from about AD 1279 to 1299, forced them to move on. Or it may have been that they were raided by other nomadic tribes that arrived in the area. Whatever the reason, the Anasazi moved away, probably joining up with other groups of Indians.

Some Hohokam sites have curious, 60-metre-long oval-shaped ball courts. These were probably used for sacred ball games similar to those found in Mexico. Players would try to pass a ball through hoops set high in the walls.

Pueblo Bonito, the 'beautiful village' of Chaco Canyon, was one of the centres of Anasazi culture. The 'ancient ones' founded a farming and trading community there which eventually grew to be one of the largest 'apartment houses' in the entire area.

The Anasazi flourished from the 9th to the 13th centuries. In this 'golden age', they built many of their amazing houses perched on the side of cliffs, and the first pueblos, or villages. Typical of these settlements were the Cliff Palace, seen in the picture below, and Pueblo Bonito, which is revealed when the see-through page is turned over.

PUEBLO BONITO

Archaeological evidence shows that Pueblo Bonito was a great house of more than 800 rooms. It was five storeys high, and terraced to catch the warmth of the sun. Within 15 kilometres of this enormous complex were a dozen similar buildings, as well as smaller villages such as Aztec pueblo. Altogether, then, Chaco society might have consisted of as many as 6,000 people. A network of simple roads linked these communities together.

THE WAY OF LIFE

The Chaco people were skilful farmers. They grew corn, squash, beans and cotton. Their fields were irrigated by a system of dams and canals, fed by the run-off water from the cliff tops around the canyon. It was the men who did most of the farming. The men also went on hunting expeditions to catch game such as deer and rabbits.

Trade was carried out both locally, with people from nearby settlements, and with some traders from far away – 'pochteca', possibly Aztecs, who visited Chaco. These men brought colourful macaws, necklaces, bracelets and other items including beautiful mosaic work. Turquoise, a valuable commodity, was often used as a form of currency.

DAILY LIFE

The houses belonged to the women, who helped to construct and maintain them. On the site were 32 ceremonial chambers called kivas (see pages 40-41). The men built, owned and maintained the kivas, and held clan meetings in them.

CLIFF DWELLINGS

Other pueblos were built on and beside the cliffs and canyon walls of the region. The cliffs protected the dwellings from the worst of the winter storms.

1 **Round tower**
2 **Sleeping room, also used as a work room in cold weather**
3 **Storeroom**
4 **Kiva**
5 **Refuse room**
6 **'Main street'**
7 **Buried ancestor**
8 **Holes for climbing to top of cliff**

CLIFF PALACE

The settlement known as the Cliff Palace, shown in the main scene, was built around AD 1100 and consists of about 220 rooms and 23 chambers called kivas. The people farmed on the clifftop above them. Cliff Palace was abandoned around 1275. Turn over the see-through page to see inside the buildings of Cliff Palace, and how the ruins appear on a modern winter's day.

SETTLERS AND RAIDERS

Although the ancient stone cities were abandoned, the Anasazi people themselves survived. They settled in new territories, and perhaps joined up with other Indian groups. Many continued to live in villages of stone or adobe houses, as they had before. They built their towns on top of the high mesas, or on flat lands close to water and their fields.

Trading at a pueblo. The Pueblo Indians would have traded turquoise and shell jewellery, baskets, pottery and blankets with the other great pueblos scattered throughout the Southwest.

PUEBLOS

When the Spanish explorer Francisco Coronado journeyed through the Rio Grande river area, he discovered small, independent villages and towns. Here the people led a peaceful way of life, farming the land, and taking part in a rich cycle of religious festivals. The Spaniards called these peoples 'pueblos', meaning 'villages' in the Spanish language.

SETTLED COMMUNITIES

By the time the Spaniards visited these villages in about 1540, their economic, political, social and ceremonial systems had become well established. These tended to be quite similar across the region, even though at least six different languages were spoken by the Pueblo Indians. It was common for the people of one pueblo to make alliances and trade with another, or for men and women to marry people from another pueblo.

THE DINEH

By the 14th century, a new Indian people had arrived in the area. They called themselves the Dineh ('People'). The Dineh were hunters who also plundered the Pueblos for food and livestock and overran their lands. But contact with the Pueblos slowly changed the Dineh's way of life. From their victims they learned farming, weaving and some religious ceremonies.

The Dineh gradually changed from a nomadic to a more settled way of life. They raised and tended flocks of sheep, goats and, later, horses stolen from the Spaniards. They did not live in towns or villages, but in settlements of hogans – small log houses – scattered over the entire territory. They grew fields of corn, and the Spaniards called them Navajo, the 'Indians of the planted fields'.

NAVAJO RAIDS

During the Spanish occupation of the Southwest, the Navajo continued to raid the white man's ranches, taking mainly horses. They did not stop until the United States acquired the area under the Treaty of Guadeloupe Hidalgo in 1848, at the end of the Mexican-American war. US forces decisively defeated the Navajo during the 1860s, driving them onto a reservation.

FIERCE WARRIORS

The Apache, whose name comes from the Zuni word meaning 'enemy', came to the Southwest around the same time as the Navajo. Like them, they raided other Indians, the Mexicans and the Spanish. However, many Apaches did not so readily settle down to become farmers. The way of life of tribes like the Jicarilla, Mescalero, Lipan and Kiowa-Apache was more like that of the Plains Indians.

The Apache were hunter-gatherers, living in camps of brushwood dwellings called 'wickiups'. After the arrival of the Spanish, they obtained more and more horses, and were able to travel long distances with ease. Soon raiding became a new way of life. The Apache were possibly the fiercest of the raiding tribes, as ruthless as the Comanche of the Plains.

This photograph is of Taos pueblo, one of the oldest inhabited pueblos, which was built sometime between AD 1300 and 1400. The word pueblo is Spanish for 'village'. Before the Spaniards arrived, there were about 90 pueblos. Today only about 30 of them are still occupied.

11

THE SPANIARDS ARRIVE

A wooden Christian cross like this one, inlaid with a mosiac, might have been worn by the first Spanish soldiers or priests who visited the Southwest.

The culture of the Southwest has long had a strong Spanish influence. This can be traced back to 1540. In that year the Spanish explorer Don Francisco Vasquez de Coronado marched north from Mexico City in search of Cibola, a mythical land with seven cities of silver and gold.

PUEBLOS

Coronado and his men searched in vain for cities of gold, although they raided Zuni and other pueblos. They eventually returned to Mexico. But interest in the land and its people did not end with their departure. Spain soon laid a permanent claim to the area, and colonization began in earnest in 1598.

Among the petroglyphs of Newspaper Rock in Utah are hunters mounted on horses. During the Spanish occupation of the Southwest, Navajos and Apaches constantly raided their ranches for horses and other loot.

CHRISTIANITY

While the Spaniards admired the large adobe dwellings, the decorated pottery, and the well-tended cotton fields of these people, there were some things about the Pueblos that they despised. In particular, they loathed the dances of the masked katchinas (see page 38) and other religious practices. They therefore set about converting the Indians to Christianity.

NEW SKILLS

The peace-loving Pueblo Indians met the Spaniards in friendship. They duly took on the new system of government and the Christian religion, although they continued to practise their own rituals in secret.

The Indians learned many skills from the newcomers. They were taught how to make iron tools, grow fruit trees and other crops, and rear cattle and sheep.

Po-pe's revolt. In secret, the people of the pueblos planned an uprising against their Spanish oppressors. At dawn on the chosen day, the Indians were to rise up and drive out the invaders. As the day drew nearer, a cord with as many knots as there were days left was passed from the organizers to each tribe. Each day, another knot was untied. When the last knot was reached the uprising began.

SPANISH RULE

The people of the pueblos were forced to swear obedience to the King of Spain and the Catholic Church. They were given Spanish names, and religious instruction by Catholic missionaries. They had to pay taxes in the form of food and textiles and provide forced labour for Spanish farms and ranches (*haciendas*). They also had to accept a new form of law, 'The Law of the Indies', which forced each village to replace its traditional priest-like lawmakers with Spanish-style officials, like governors and lieutenant-governors.

The Spaniards also tried to convert the nomadic Apache and Navajo. Some of these were forced into slavery in Spanish mines. The Apache and Navajo put up a fierce resistance to the invaders. This put them at even greater odds with the Pueblo Indians, with whom they had sometimes been on friendly terms in pre-conquest times. Raids on the pueblos became more common, since they were now seen as allies of the Spaniards.

The first Spaniard to see a pueblo said it was as big as a city and full of treasure. Francisco Coronado's quest for this treasure took him from Mexico through the Southwest and on to the Plains. Still having seen no cities of gold, he despaired and turned back. This scene shows Coronado in battle.

THE GREAT REBELLION OF 1680

As Spanish oppression increased, the situation for the native peoples became unbearable. A long period of drought made the situation even worse. To the Indians, these factors seemed to symbolize that the delicate balance between humans and nature had been upset.

This so angered a Tewa Medicine Man, Po-pe, that he devised a plan to drive the Spanish out. After four years of planning so that the people would fight together, the revolt went ahead. It was a complete success. The uprising took the Spanish totally by surprise. In spite of their superior firepower, they were driven south as far as El Paso, Texas. Po-pe became a virtual dictator and tried to wipe out all Spanish influence.

THE SPANISH RETURN

The Spanish were not easily beaten, however. In 1693 they returned and quickly reconquered 'New Mexico', as it came to be called. Again, the Indians seemed to accept Spanish domination, but as before, the secret practice of ancient religious ceremonies went on. By this time, Po-pe had died and the general wish of the people was to avoid further conflict and bloodshed.

Spanish-style blacksmithing in Zuni pueblo. The smiths used hand-operated 'concertina' bellows and a wrought iron anvil. The forge was made of adobe bricks lined with stones. An alcove above the fire allowed the smoke to escape.

TRIBAL GOVERNMENT

Apache religion included powerful and important members of a band known as holy, or medicine, men. This picture is of a medicine man of the Mescalero Apaches, called Gorgonio. The picture is based on a photograph by A. Frank Randall, who visited the Southwest in the 1880s.

Long before the white man arrived on the scene, the Indian nations of the South-west had developed their own systems of government. Each pueblo was an independent community and each had its own religious rituals and social code.

FAMILIES AND CLANS

The Southwestern Indians did not think of families being only two parents and their children. Families were extended to include other relatives on both the father's and mother's side, and were called 'clans'.

Clan loyalties were very important. The Navajo, for example, were divided into over 50 clans who traced their descent through their mother's rather than their father's family. Clan names might come from a particular tribe or group, as with the Zuni, or they might be named after the spirit of an animal, as with the Hopi.

COUNCILS

Traditionally, each pueblo was led by a council of between 10 and 30 members. The council officials included the kiva priests (see page 40), a war chief, who enforced the pueblo's laws, and also a ceremonial officer who was the pueblo's spiritual leader, or *cacique* as he was called in Spanish. The *cacique* was chosen for life.

Under Spanish rule, the King of Spain ordered that a governor and lieutenant-governor should also be made part of the government. The peaceful Indians obeyed, incorporating the new officers into their council. This system still survives in the pueblos today.

SPIRITUAL GUIDANCE

The Pueblo Indians believed that their leaders were guided by divine spirits. The council directed all community events, including hunts, medical matters and the defence of the pueblo itself.

Tribal ceremonies were always led by the *cacique*. Occasionally, the council acted as a court of law, judging people accused of crimes, such as witchcraft.

Each Hopi clan had its own special stories and ceremonies that were important in the life of the tribe as a whole. Among the most important Hopi clans were the Bear, Parrot and Eagle clans. These men are preparing for a Buffalo Dance ceremony. One is making a sun symbol from eagle feathers. It will be worn by an unmarried Hopi woman. The other is making a headdress for the male dancers.

This photograph, taken in the 1880s, shows Naite, the chief of the Apache on the San Carlos reservation. He has a short-handled riding whip on a thong around his wrist.

Within the council itself, all decisions had to be agreed unanimously. Pueblo communities worked on the principle of co-operation – they frowned on individuals who did not work for the community. Almost everybody obeyed the rules. When they did not, decisions could be enforced either through the *cacique* or through a powerful demonstration of divine will by the katchinas (see page 38).

THE PIMA AND PAPAGO

Tribal organization was strong among the Pima, who had a single leader elected by the headmen of the villages. The Papago were also governed by headmen, selected for their personal qualities, and by councils of all the adult males. The elders in each council dominated meetings, while young men were expected to maintain a respectful silence. Decisions were made only by unanimous agreement. The seeking of personal power was frowned upon.

THE APACHE

Unlike the Pueblo Indians, the Pima and the Papago, the Apache had no form of tribal government. They were organized into 'bands'. These were independent groups of families, often related to each other, who worked, fought and travelled together. Each band was led by a chief who made decisions for the group, such as when they should move from place to place, and when hunts, ceremonies and other activities would take place.

The chief was expected to be brave, strong and wise. His power was limited to essentially that of an advisor, though. At any time, a family that was dissatisfied with his leadership could leave the group and join another. Sometimes the chiefship was hereditary, held by a single family or clan.

THE NAVAJO

Navajo government was similar to that of the Apache. Each local band had a single leader, or *natani*, who served for life, as well as one or more war chiefs.

Tribal organization was introduced in the 1920s, when the Navajo set up a general council, mainly to deal more effectively with the US government. In time, this became the tribal council of today.

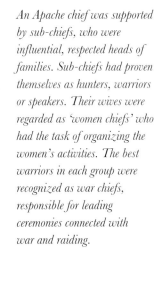

An Apache chief was supported by sub-chiefs, who were influential, respected heads of families. Sub-chiefs had proven themselves as hunters, warriors or speakers. Their wives were regarded as 'women chiefs' who had the task of organizing the women's activities. The best warriors in each group were recognized as war chiefs, responsible for leading ceremonies connected with war and raiding.

A PUEBLO

The Pueblo Indians get their name from their villages of permanent homes, built out of mud and/or stone. Some of these were built a long time before the white man set foot in the region, and a few are still inhabited today.

BUILDINGS

Pueblos comprised large, flat-roofed buildings, rectangular or oval in shape and often several storeys high. The storeys were built in terraced layers and resembled blocks of flats. They were usually made of stone or mud. Each pueblo was laid out around a small network of streets and a number of spacious plazas.

CONSTRUCTION

The building of a mud pueblo began with the construction of thick walls. These mud walls were then covered with adobe – a mixture of clay and straw which became very hard when it dried. Adobe is a brownish-grey colour, which meant that the pueblo buildings blended well into their surroundings. The roof of the pueblo was made from wooden poles and branches, covered with earth and grass, and supported inside by huge log 'vigas'.

The entrance to each dwelling was through an opening in the roof, reached using pole ladders. These could be removed from below and stored inside in the event of an enemy attack, particularly from raiding bands of Navajo and Apache.

STREETS AND PLAZAS

One typical feature of the village were large circular ovens situated outside the dwellings themselves. These were used for making bread, and were probably introduced by the Spaniards.

1 **Entrance through roof**
2 **Small window**
3 **'Bee-hive' oven**
4 **Walls of adobe, sun-dried bricks**
5 **Hearth with fire**
6 **Chimney to draw out smoke**
7 **Building a new room**
8 **Plastering the pueblo walls**

FREQUENT REPAIRS

The adobe buildings needed constant care and maintenance to prevent them from disintegrating in the rain. The adobe had to be renewed regularly, and the earth roofs patched and repaired. Much of this work was done by family groups or by the whole community. It was usually the women who applied the mud plastering, forming and smoothing it, and then using a sheepskin to give it a final finish.

'Do not forget your house.
Here in your own house
You will always go about happily.
Always talking together kindly
We shall pass our days.'

Zuni saying

The see-through scene below shows a generalised pueblo. Each of the dwellings is entered through the roof. Note the traditional small windows, so that raiders cannot break in through them. Pueblos also had kivas (see pages 40-41). A few buildings in this pueblo have doors, a relatively modern feature: the villagers must feel secure from attack.

THE FAMILY

Children were given items to help them understand tribal traditions and ceremonies. Hopi parents gave their children wooden figures dressed as katchina dancers to help them learn to recognise each katchina and its characteristics. This is a rain katchina: its eyes represent rain clouds and its lashes the rain.

The family was central to daily life throughout the Southwest. Men and women shared in some tasks, such as house-building, but in other activities there was often a fairly rigid division of labour. From a very young age, children were taught tribal beliefs and values and encouraged to become strong and useful members of society.

'Puva, puva, puva,
In the trail the beetles
On each other's backs are sleeping
So on mine, my baby, thou
Puva, puva, puva!'

— *Hopi lullaby* —

THE DIVISION OF LABOUR

It was the Apache and Navajo men who planted and tilled the fields and gathered firewood. They looked after the horses and cattle, went out on raids and hunts, and prepared the skins of the animals they had killed. They also made their own bows, arrows and shields. Women cared for the children, prepared and cooked the meals, made pottery, wove blankets and performed other duties around the house.

Pueblo men constructed the houses and ceremonial kivas, but the women did the plastering with adobe. The children were expected to help out, too. Navajo boys and girls collected wood for the fire and went out each day with the sheep.

THE WOMAN'S ROLE

Although the role of the woman was primarily domestic, she traditionally held a very important place in society. This was reinforced through myths and folklore. Some of the most important spirits (see page 38) are female.

In early days, all the belongings of the family, apart from personal items, such as clothing, jewellery, ceremonial equipment and saddles, were the property of the women. However, the land and natural resources, such as water or timber, belonged to neither men nor women, but were held in 'trusteeship' by both sexes.

An Apache baby spent most of its first year tied in a cradleboard.

GOOD BEHAVIOUR

Pueblo children in particular were taught to be modest and to avoid violence. Parents treated their children considerately, but warned of punishment by the spirits if they misbehaved. Very naughty children were sent to the village disciplinarians, who wore frightening masks. On Tewa pueblo, these persons would make the children dance while cracking whips at their heels. Members of the Clown societies might also make fun of naughty children.

When an Apache girl reached puberty, she performed the Sunrise Dance. She was dressed to represent Changing Woman, an important mythological figure whom she symbolically became (see page 37). She was assisted by a sponsor, a woman who had to be of good reputation.

During the Apache Sunrise ceremony, masked dancers wearing tall headdresses called crowns impersonate protective mountain spirits known as 'gans'. The dancers call on the power of the mountain spirits to drive away evil, to cure sickness and bring good fortune.

CHILDHOOD

The birth of a child was always celebrated, often by performing a special ceremony. On Tewa pueblo, a newborn child was taken out, presented to the rising Sun and given a name. Afterwards, at regular intervals in the child's life, he or she would be instructed in tribal ways, and they would take part in certain rituals to prepare for adulthood.

EARLY TRAINING

A Pueblo boy would go into the kiva for an introduction to the katchinas and lengthy training in the rites and duties of the kiva society. An Apache boy would train as a warrior and a hunter. His first important expedition was usually as a member of a raiding party. Every Apache girl underwent an important puberty ceremony – the Sunrise Dance – which marked her entry into womanhood.

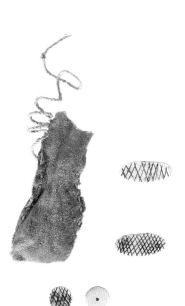

We know that the Anasazi played games with counters, like this set found complete with its leather carrying bag.

19

This beautiful shell ornament dates from about AD 1000. To make it, a Hohokam craftworker first coated parts of the shell with a tar-like substance. Then he or she used an acid made from the fermented juice of a saguaro cactus to eat away the uncovered parts of the shell.

The Indians of the Southwest were mainly farmers. However, they did not rely on farming alone for their food. They also gathered wild fruits and berries, hunted game, and kept livestock.

CLIMATE

The climate of the Southwest is very dry, and water is precious. Very little rain falls on the desert; sometimes there is none at all for a whole year. When the rain does come, it usually falls in short but heavy storms which can cause considerable damage. Also, most of the region is at high altitude (1,500 metres). The growing season is therefore limited by late frosts in the spring and early frosts in the winter.

For this reason most Pueblo Indians lived in villages and farmed along rivers or streams that had enough water to irrigate their crops. Some other tribes lived in villages, but moved from place to place with the changing seasons. The Mohave caught river fish, using long-handled nets made of woven willow twigs. Other tribes were essentially hunter-gathers, such as the Apache. They moved about in small bands in search of food.

Papago women gathered wild foods, such as grass seeds and mesquite beans, and also the fruits of the huge saguaro cactus which were used to make jam, syrup and ritual wine.

Apache women gather flowers from yucca plants. One of the women is carrying her baby in a cradleboard strapped to her back; another has a large burden basket, used when harvesting large quantities of food or fruit.

FARMING

Tribes like the Hopi and Zuni practised 'dry land farming' by siting their fields where they could take best advantage of rain running off from the cliffs. Others used purpose-built irrigation canals to collect and divert water to their fields.

CROPS

The primary crops were corn, beans, squash and cotton. Later, the Spaniards introduced wheat, alfafa, chilli and fruit – peach, plum, apple and cherry. Herbs were collected and used in ceremonies, or made into household medicines. Corn was such an important food that the Indians worshipped it. Throughout the year they held ceremonies to bring rain and make their crops grow.

PLANTING

Spring was the time of planting. Men did all the work in the fields, using wooden digging sticks and hoes. Harvesting was done in the autumn. The wheat was first cut with sickles, then taken to an enclosure with a hardened adobe floor. It was then trampled by goats and horses to separate the wheat from the chaff.

HUNTING AND GATHERING

The Navajo and the Apache both learned some farming from the Pueblo Indians, but they depended chiefly on gathering wild fruits and edible plants, and hunting deer, pronghorn antelope and rabbits. Groups of men stalked their prey and drove it into stockades or pits. The women gathered pinon pine nuts, berries and cacti, and yucca fruit.

SHEEP AND CATTLE

The Navajo learned sheep-rearing from the Spaniards. Sheep and goats were important to the Navajo, because they provided both meat and wool. The latter was made into clothing, rugs and blankets for their own use or to trade or sell. Ownership of livestock was also a sign of wealth and importance. It was usually the responsibility of the women and children to take care of the herd.

Winnowing was carried out by farmers in enclosures about 10 metres across. These enclosures were surrounded by stakes or a wooden fence.

21

APACHE LIFE

A typical scene in an Apache camp. The woman in front of the wickiup is fleshing a deerhide, with a tool made from elk or deer bone, while the children watch out for the returning hunting party.

Apache warriors gather around a fire at night-time. The picture is from a painting by Frederic Remington, whose evocative and dramatic paintings of the American West are famous throughout the world.

The Apache were a fierce, nomadic peoples, who arrived in the Southwest around AD 1000 following the migrating buffalo herds. They were not one distinct nation, but were divided into a number of separate tribes – the Jicarilla, Mescalero, Chiricahua, Kiowa-Apache and Lipan. They were influenced both by the settled Pueblo Indians and their nomadic neighbours on the Plains.

HUNTER-GATHERERS
The Apache were essentially hunter-gatherers, although the Jicarilla and the Lipan also did some farming. Men hunted in groups, killing deer, antelope and rabbits. Hunting was something they excelled at, often riding hard over long distances in pursuit of their prey.

A WOMAN'S ROLE
Like their neighbours on the Plains, Apache women were expected to tan hides, sew leather and make clothes. They also gathered wild foods such as pinon pine nuts, mesquite and mescal heads, from a type of cactus. (The name Mescalero comes from the Apache custom of gathering and roasting heads of mescal.)

Among the Apache tribes that practised agriculture, women farmed the crops too – corn, beans and squash in particular. They were also responsible for running the camp, such as cooking the food and gathering fuel for the camp fires.

This beautifully painted deerskin depicts an Apache ritual dance. The Apache were the most nomadic of the Indians of the Southwest, and therefore their art was usually expressed in practical items that could easily be carried.

WICKIUPS

Each Apache tribe was made up of an independent group of families, all related to one another. Each tribal group lived in scattered camps of round, brushwood-covered dwellings called 'wickiups'. In hot weather, they moved outside to open-air shelters with brush and grass roofs – called 'remadas' – set up near the wickiups.

Wickiups were circular, conical or dome-shaped houses. They were usually constructed by the women out of mesquite, cottonwood or willow poles bound with yucca plant fibre and covered with brush and bear grass. In cold weather wickiups might be covered tightly with skins that could be rolled up and removed in warm weather. Some wickiups were large and roomy; others small temporary shelters.

An Apache warclub, consisting of a stone head, a wooden handle covered with rawhide, and a horsehair tail.

BOLD RAIDERS

The Apache were bold, clever raiders who used surprise attacks to steal horses, cattle and other loot. Raids on other Indians, the Spaniards and, later, the Mexicans and Anglo-American settlers, made them much feared throughout the Southwest.

RELIGION

The Apache believed religion was both a personal and community matter. Power might be obtained from a personal vision and then shared with the rest of society. A person who did this was a shaman. The shaman – a man or woman – would carry out ceremonies for the sick, and play an essential part in major rituals. From the Pueblos, the Apache adopted the practice of using 'clowns' and masked dancers in their ceremonies.

WITCHCRAFT

Illness and misfortune were often believed to be caused by witchcraft. Many Apaches believed in ghosts and witches, and felt the need for protection against them. It was customary for the home and possessions of a person who had died to be burned and the site of death abandoned.

A young Apache warrior hunts an antelope. The hunting of large game animals was the responsibility of the men. Training began in childhood, when boys were taught the rules and rituals required to become skilful and successful hunters.

NAVAJO HOGANS

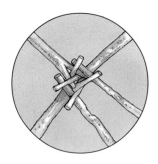

The framework of a traditional forked-pole hogan consists of three interlocking forked poles plus two other poles that extend from the entrance.

The see-through scene below shows some of the main types of hogan built by the Navajo.

The other raiders of the Southwest were the Navajo. However, influenced by the Pueblo Indians, they soon settled to a more peaceful life of farming. The traditional Navajo home was called a 'hogan'.

MULTI-PURPOSE HOMES

The hogan was a low, dome-shaped structure with walls made of logs, cemented with clay and mud, and covered in earth. It was warm inside in winter yet cool in summer. Hogans were not built in towns or villages, but scattered across Navajo land in dispersed settlements.

A family often had more than one hogan, each for a different purpose – one for living, one mainly for storage and another for healing ceremonies.

STRUCTURE

Ancient hogans were cone-shaped, forked-stick structures. They had a foundation of three upright poles locked together at the top. Two poles were laid up against the forks at the east side to form the doorway. The whole structure was covered with earth, apart from the doorway and a smokehole at the top. Navajo sweat lodges are still built in this fashion.

The more familiar modern hogan was the six-sided 'cribbed log' hogan. This was built by making a frame out of four forked posts set in the ground and placing layers of logs, one on top of another, to form the familiar dome-shape. Again, the whole structure was covered with earth.

BUILDING A HOGAN

Around the hogans were other structures. There were shades, open-air sun shelters like those also used by the Apache, as well as lamb pens and corrals for the animals, outdoor ovens, and a sweat lodge some distance away.

1 **Cribbed log hogan**
2 **Smoke hole**
3 **Hearth below smoke hole**
4 **Ceremonial 'hogan with legs'**
5 **Forked-pole hogan, the oldest form of hogan**
6 **Sweat lodge, for purifying baths**
7 **Lean-to shelter, or shade**

SPECIAL PLACES

The hogan was built to traditional rules. The fire was placed in the centre and doorways faced east towards the rising sun.

People slept and sat around the fire, with everyone having their own place. Men sat on the north side, women on the south. Guests, and other important persons, such as shamans, or priests, sat on the west side facing the doorway. Herbs, dried foods, weapons, ceremonial equipment and clothes were stored up in the rafters or suspended from beams. Pots and pans were stacked around the fire.

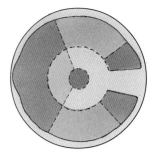

Different parts of a hogan are given names by the Navajo, including the northern, southern and western recesses (top, bottom and left in the diagram), as well as the hearth (centre), the 'area between the fire and the western wall', and the fireside.

CLOTHING AND DECORATION

Some Hohokam sandals and baskets have survived in the dry mountain air of the Southwest. These sandals were woven from yucca fibre.

Men and women of the Yuma and Mohave painted their faces, and often tattooed their chins. Tattooing was sometimes done to increase a person's beauty, but it was often inspired by dreams and therefore had a personal, spiritual meaning.

The clothing of the first peoples of the Southwest was made from fur, buckskin, feathers and cotton. After the introduction of sheep by the Spaniards, wool was used to make garments such as cloaks, and blankets. Turquoise and silver jewellery was popular with many men and women in the region.

PUEBLAN CLOTHING

The Pueblo Indians spun yarn from cotton and wove it into cloth on looms. There were two main types – the small belt loom was used by the men to make ceremonial sashes, while the wide vertical loom, brought by the Spaniards, was used to make clothes.

Pueblo men's clothing usually consisted of cotton breechcloths and kilts. Women wore a piece of cloth around their bodies, fastened under the left arm and over the right shoulder. On their legs, they wore buckskin wrappings that reached down to the top of their moccasins. Later, clothing was made from woollen cloth. The Yuman, whose homelands were among the hottest in the area, did not need much clothing. Men often wore only narrow breechcloths, and women aprons that covered both front and back.

Many items of clothing were decorated with beadwork. This simple, fringed buckskin shirt would have been worn by a child for everyday use.

THE RAIDERS

Early Apache and Navajo clothing was made of animal skins. Men wore breechcloths with long sleeved shirts, women two-piece dresses or skirts. The Navajo later adopted loom-weaving and Pueblo-style clothing.

Navajo women, in particular, were famed for their bright garments. In the 19th century, with the introduction of European fabrics, Navajo women adopted their own distinctive costume of velveteen blouses and full calico skirts. They still wear these today.

The hair of young Navajo girls was traditionally combed with a hairbrush made of a tied bundle of grass stems (left). Hopi girls' hair was woven around a wooden hair bow into a whorl. This formed the 'squash blossom' style seen below.

COLD-WEATHER WEAR

In cold weather, all peoples wore blankets or ponchos. At first, these were made out of rabbit skins sewn together or hide. The blankets of the Apache had a long fringe, and were woven in a solid colour. Boot leggings made out of thick hide were also worn to keep out the cold. These were decorated with silver or beadwork.

When wool was introduced, Navajo women adopted the Spanish custom of weaving 'serapes' (shawls), decorated with patterns of diamonds, triangles and stripes.

This pair of Mescalero Apache legging moccasins is highly decorated with beadwork, brass beads and metal buttons. The leggings are made of soft buckskin while the soles are made of much tougher rawhide.

HAIR-STYLES

The Indians took great care with their hair. They used plants such as the cactus to make hair tonics and washes. Hair was usually worn long, and combed back into various styles. Sometimes, a style was worn to show tribal status. The 'squash blossom' style, for example, was worn by unmarried Pueblo girls. Hair was sometimes wrapped in a cloth. Navajo men often wore a wide band of cloth or a scarf as a headband. Women, on the other hand, would wear a piece of cloth like a cap, covering the head and tied behind.

During ceremonies, people usually wore their hair loose, although a high-ranking warrior, particularly among the Apache, usually wore a special fancy headdress or decorated cap.

In the 19th century, watch fobs were considered fashionable by Apache men. The design of the red one is inspired by the flag of the USA, the green one has a deer motif.

27

BASKETRY AND POTTERY

Stylized flowers, birds or animals, like the deer on this Zuni water jar, were popular decorations on Zuni pots, particularly in the 19th century.

The Southwest has a long tradition of art and craft, reaching back as much as 12,000 years to the very first civilizations. These traditions have seen much development and change over the centuries as various influences from outside have been absorbed. Indian baskets, pottery, rugs, jewellery and carving are famous to this day, and are much sought after.

BASKETRY

Early examples of basketware have been found in the caves inhabited by the Anasazi. Some were so tightly woven they could hold water! Apache women were particularly skilled at basketry, making carrying and storage baskets and bowls that were both useful and beautiful. They used willow and cotton wood to form wicker, plaited or coiled baskets, and they obtained natural dyes from plants. Early decorations were mainly geometric shapes, whirls and crosses. In the 19th century, more realistic motifs such as horses and dogs became popular.

The other nations of the Southwest had their own basket-making traditions, and although the development of pottery reduced the use of baskets among the pueblos, the Hopi have preserved the tradition to this day.

This Zuni potter is using a technique called coil pottery. Pieces of clay are formed into long thin rolls, and then carefully used to build up the shape of the pot.

An Apache woman weaving a finely-coiled basket tray, probably for household use, such as mixing, winnowing or serving. She is softening the plant fibres using water kept in the small pan beside her.

POTTERY

Pottery, another ancient Indian craft, evolved naturally from basketry. Somewhere between AD 400 and 700, the Indians of the Southwest began using open baskets as moulds. They lined them with clay, forming the pot, and left it to dry. Pottery was usually made by the women.

In time, the coil method of pottery evolved. This consisted of building up the sides of the pot with successive coils of rolled clay, and then smoothing it evenly with a tool or smoothing stone. Simple kilns were also developed to fire the pottery, making it possible to produce watertight pots in many different shapes and sizes for use in cooking and storage.

SPANISH INFLUENCE

Pueblo pottery changed rapidly after the Spanish conquest. The Spanish were impressed with the quality and the beauty of the pottery they saw, and traded with the pueblos for great quantities of it. The potters started to make new, untraditional items for their customers, either for domestic use or for use in churches. These included candlesticks and even baptismal fonts.

Pottery designs too were influenced by Spanish taste, particularly for floral patterns, and the Moorish eight-pointed star. In the 19th century, white traders moved into the area and opened up new markets for the potters.

Each pueblo painted pottery with its own unique designs. Zia pueblo, for example, preferred sky, bird and cloud motifs, while Santa Domingo specialized in geometric designs.

Firing pottery. Unfired pots were placed on a sheet of metal or a grate to separate them from the ground.

Sometimes, a technique called 'smudging' was used. When the fire was hot, it was covered with mashed manure or straw, thus making a thick smoke which turned the pots black. When the firing was complete, the pots were removed from the ashes and wiped off.

The pots were then surrounded by pieces of broken pots, or sheets of metal, to prevent them from burning. Blocks of manure or wood were the most common fuel. They were stacked around the pottery and lit.

The fetish necklace, like this example from Zuni pueblo, is often made of small shell birds combined with stone or shell beads.

Weaving is an ancient craft, dating back some **9,000** years, when Indians wove rush mats and sandals. For a time, weaving was primarily the task of the men, because it was seen as a sacred occupation. Inside kivas, ceremonial pieces such as sashes for katchinas were woven or sewn from yucca plant fibre, cotton, rabbit fur and feathers.

WEAVING

Wool was introduced when the Spaniards brought sheep to the area, around 1600. It was readily adopted, particularly by the Navajo, who probably learned weaving from the Pueblo Indians. Navajo women began to spin the wool and weave it on upright 'vertical' looms.

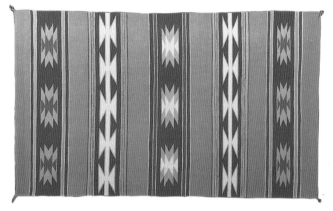

The Navajo not only used blankets themselves, but sold or bartered them to other Indians and settlers. Then, in the late 19th century, pressure from white traders encouraged the production of the famous rugs, instead of blankets. The blanket at the top has a simple geometric pattern, whereas the rug below it depicts two holy people and a maize plant.

PATTERNS

The Navajo became renowned for their many different styles of weave and their intricate, striped designs. They used natural black and white wool, mixing them to produce grey. They also experimented with dyes obtained from plants and earth to make different colours – yellow, blue, green and red. Red was especially popular, and came from cochineal, extracted from the bodies of scale insects.

A Navajo weaver sits at her large rectangular, upright loom. It is made from four wooden beams lashed together and set in the ground.

This Apache tobacco canteen, made of buffalo rawhide, copies a style of canteen made in silver by the Mexicans and Navajo in the mid-19th century. It would also be worn as a necklace.

KATCHINAS

The Hopi, Zuni and other Pueblo Indians carved katchina figures, or dolls as they are sometimes called, although they are not dolls in the conventional sense. There are many katchinas, each representing a supernatural being closely connected with customs, religious belief and tribal history. Katchina figures ranged in size from a few centimetres to more than 30 cm, and were carved by men from the roots of sacred cottonwood trees.

Katchina figures were usually given protruding eyes and ears, beaklike mouths and noses and elaborate headdresses. They were painted in vivid colours – white, red, blue or green and black. These colours were traditionally obtained from plants, although when traders introduced opaque watercolours and poster paints, these were readily adopted. Colour was often of spiritual significance.

Like the katchinas themselves, katchina masks can represent the sky, stars, clouds, lightning, animals, birds and supernatural beings. This one, in painted leather, represents the earth and sky beings.

TURQUOISE

The Zuni were fine jewellers who specialized in inlay work. They used turquoise, as well as coral and other stones, in their jewellery. But perhaps the finest jewellers were the Navajo, who used metals such as iron and copper to make bracelets, necklaces, rings and earrings. They were particularly skilled in setting stones such as turquoise in their jewellery.

The Southwest area was rich in turquoise, mined from rock deposits in Arizona, New Mexico and Colorado. Turquoise was highly valued not only for its beauty, but because it was believed to offer protection against evil.

SILVERSMITHS

The Navajo's first contact with silver-smithing occurred when they saw Spanish craftsmen at work. They were fascinated by the beauty of this new metal, and silver ornaments became prized booty in raids. In the 19th century, the Navajo learned the art of silversmithing from Mexicans, and they were soon creating jewellery from American and Mexican coins.

Many jewellery designs, such as the famous 'squash blossom', were based on the leaves and flowers of the maize plant, the squash, the pomegranate and the pumpkin. Another common design was the horseshoe-shaped 'naja', actually an ancient Moorish symbol the Spaniards used to decorate their horses' bridles.

Silverworking began in earnest when the Navajo were imprisoned in Bosque Redondo after the notorious 'Long Walk' (see page 43). They also mastered the art of setting stones at this time, a skill they taught to the Zuni. This craftsman is using a pump drill, a device for making holes in flat turquoise and shell beads.

DANCE AND MUSIC

The Shalako dancers wore costumes that made them look like tall, wingless birds with long black clacking beaks.

Dancing always meant something special to the Indians of the Southwest. It expressed their attitude to life, their relationship with nature, and their place among other people.

SEASONAL DANCES

Pueblo dances were held on many occasions throughout the year, according to the changing seasons. They were usually performed in the pueblo plazas, whilst people watched from the roofs.

Careful preparations were the key to the proper execution of the dance. All the colours and details of the costumes had to be right, the dance steps had to be precise, and the choruses and chants had to be rhythmic and appropriate to the ceremony. Traditionally, the songs and dance steps used in ritual were carefully taught to the boys when they were old enough to join the secret meetings in the kivas.

TRIBAL DANCES

Each tribe had its own dances, performed for a variety of reasons. Some dances were dazzling displays of skill and endurance. More often than not, they had a religious significance. There were, for example, dances to make the rain fall, to make the corn grow, to thank the spirits for good crops, and to cure sickness. Other dances honoured birds and animals. Some told stories and legends, or related the history of the pueblo. Many of the dances are carried out today, as they have been for hundreds of years.

THE SNAKE DANCE

There were many famous dances. The Snake Dance, so hated by the Spanish invaders, was a rain dance. Deep in a kiva, a Snake Priest would dance on the altar, holding a live snake in his mouth. After the ceremonies, the snakes would be carried to specially chosen places and released with a request to bring rain.

An Apache drum and beater. The drum is made of skin stretched over a wooden frame, and would have been used to accompany singers and dancers.

This painting on an Anasazi kiva wall shows a dancer. Paintings have been found on kiva walls that date back to the 11th century.

32

ZUNI DANCES

The Zuni performed a whole series of spectacular masked dances, culminating in the great winter ceremony, the 'Shalako'. The Shalako were believed to be the messengers of katchina spirits. They would come into the pueblo to dance in the Shalako houses, built especially for them.

SONGS

Like dances, songs were sung either as part of a ritual, or purely for pleasure. The Navajo had songs for many occasions. There were lullabies, children's songs, comic songs and songs like 'Gift Songs' for an exchange of presents. There were also various dancing songs, like the Circle Song, sung as the people danced around in a circle. Then there were the many ceremonial songs and chants from the 'sings' (see pages 39).

Almost all singing was accompanied by a drum. Cedar-wood flutes too were popular. Other instruments included clay pipes and rattles. The Navajo 'singer' or one of his helpers used a special rattle called a 'bullroarer' or 'groaning stick'. This was traditionally made from a piece of wood taken from a tree that had been struck by lightning. When it was twirled, the rattle made a sound like thunder.

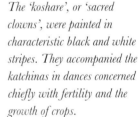

The 'koshare', or 'sacred clowns', were painted in characteristic black and white stripes. They accompanied the katchinas in dances concerned chiefly with fertility and the growth of crops.

On Taos pueblo, the Deer Dance was led by the Deer Mother, carefully chosen by the spiritual leaders of the pueblo. In this dance, the men wore the hides and horns of the deer that they had taken during the hunting season.

33

DEATH AND BURIAL

Among the Navajo, death and everything connected with it was terrible. They would not touch a corpse, and often burned the hogan of the dead person and everything in it, believing that it had become contaminated.

All the Indians of the Southwest had strong beliefs about death and the afterlife. People feared that ghosts might return home and haunt the living, so they performed elaborate ceremonies to keep the living from harm. The Apache, Pima and Navajo burned the property of the dead. The Apache also believed that animals such as coyotes, bears and owls could contain the ghosts of witches and other restless spirits.

FUNERAL CEREMONIES

In their funeral ceremonies, the Pueblos helped mourners forget the dead and not grieve too much. On Zuni pueblo, as soon as a death occurred, the officiating priest would cut off a lock of the dead person's hair. He would then scatter sacred cornmeal to make a symbolic road to separate the mourners from their grief.

BANISHING THE SPIRIT

The Pueblo Indians believed that the spirit, or 'wind', of the deceased remained in his or her home for four days after death. On the fourth day, the priest would build an altar, on which he put prayer sticks, the dead person's possessions, a bowl of medicine water and a basket of food. He then made another cornmeal road, sprinkled the relatives with water to purify them and opened the house door. Finally, he spoke to the dead person, inviting him or her to sit down and eat for the last time before being sent away.

CHASING THE DEAD

Afterwards, everything used in the ceremony was buried outside the village, and the mourners symbolically chased the dead away along the cornmeal road. The door was then bolted against the spirit of the departed.

perhaps as an animal, such as an owl or coyote. They inhabited the land of the dead – a fearful shadowy place over which the living had no control at all.

BURIAL IN THE HILLS

The customs of the Apache were very different. When a death occurred, they publicly wept, wailed and cut their hair, much like the Plains peoples. The body of a deceased Apache was ceremonially washed and dressed in his finest clothes, and placed on his favourite horse, with as many of his personal possessions as it could carry. A burial party led the horse and its burden far away into hilly country to find a suitable rock crevice that would serve as a grave.

On the Feast of the Dead, Pueblan women offer gifts to their dead relatives. They put bowls containing food on the graves and light candles around them.

WHITE CLOUD MASK

The Hopi believed that the dead were reborn into a new world, so many of their ceremonies were similar to those performed for a newborn child. They washed the face and body of the dead person with cornmeal, made prayer sticks and even gave the person a new name. Then they tied feathers over the head, painted the face black and put a cotton mask, a 'white cloud mask', over it. This was to make the body 'light' like a cloud and able to breathe in another world.

GHOSTS AND WITCHES

Unless a person died naturally, death was often believed to be the result of witchcraft. Many Indians believed in ghosts and the power of witches, and felt the need for protection against them. The Navajo saw ghosts as lonely spirits, who might return from the land of the dead to seek more spirits, to avenge an old quarrel or for some reason of neglect. For example, a ghost might return if its corpse had not been buried properly or its grave had been disturbed.

However kind and friendly a person may have been when they were alive, their ghost was a potential danger to the living. Only the spirits of those who had died either very old or very young were believed to be harmless. Ghosts appeared in the dark, sometimes in human form or

Apaches lead the horse of a dead warrior into the hills. Some of the dead warrior's possessions will be buried with him, the rest will be broken or burned. His horse will also be killed to accompany its owner into the spirit world.

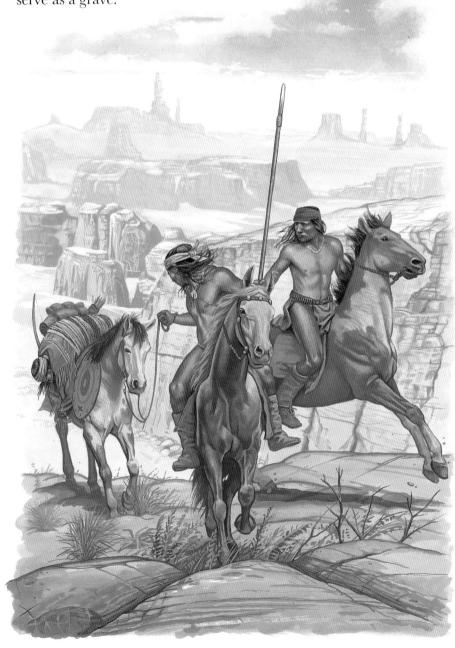

35

MYTHS AND LEGENDS

This water vessel is in the form of an owl. Animals and birds are common in Zuni mythology.

The early peoples of the Southwest had two types of rock art: petroglyphs, drawings on stone that were carved or scratched into the rock, and pictographs, which were usually painted in shades of red onto the rock surface. The decorated rocks often mark sacred sites that tell the history of the early Indian peoples.

The Indians loved to listen to folktales, myths and legends. Families often gathered around the fireside to listen to tales. The tales were meant to teach, as well as to entertain, being closely connected with the peoples' religious beliefs and traditions.

THE TELLING OF STORIES

Legends of gods, spirits and ancestors were handed down from father to son. These included stories of the world before it had people, stories of the origin of the people and tribes, and tales of tribal heroes.

Stories were usually told by a special storyteller, but important myths were danced or sung. The 'Great Dreams' of the Yuma people, for example, were often dramatically recited to audiences. Stories were also told in signs and pictures on rocks and on the walls of canyons. They were never written down, though, because the Indians did not have a system of writing like ours.

These two figures representing gods are from a fresco on a kiva wall in New Mexico. They date from the mid-15th century. Avan Yu, top, is the snake of the underworld. The snake appears in stories told all over the Southwest. He is believed to be a healer and to bring rain to the desert. Ko-Lo-Wissi, above, is the god of the plumed serpent. The plumed or feathered serpent is one of the chief gods of Mexican peoples, such as the Maya and Aztecs.

Southwestern legend tells how the sons of Changing Woman and her husband, the Sun, helped to destroy monsters who troubled the Earth, including the Swallower of Clouds.

TYPES OF MYTH

Among the major types of myth were creation myths, which explain how the world and its inhabitants were first made; emergence myths, which tell how the people emerged from past worlds into the present one; and hero myths, which relate the exploits of a hero. The First Beings and ancestors, who often appear in these tales, are teachers who show the Indians skills such as weaving, and instruct them how to carry out ceremonies.

In the Hopi creation story, Tawa the Sky God and Grandmother Spider make the Earth and everything and everyone on it. Grandmother Spider has the job of putting the world in order, so she makes and names all the different Indian nations. She separates the tribes into clans and chooses an animal to lead each one. This, the Hopi say, explains the clan structure of their people. Hopi clans are still led by their clan animal to this day.

EMERGING FROM THE EARTH

Navajo emergence myths describe how the Holy People once lived below the surface of the Earth. They were forced to move from one underground world to another by the witchcraft of one of their own members. Finally, a great flood drove the Holy People to ascend to the present world through a reed.

THE HERO TWINS

Changing Woman is an important being in many Southwestern myths. In one Navajo hero myth, she gives birth to twin sons – the Hero Twins – who journey to the house of their father, the Sun. They have many adventures and slay numerous monsters along the way.

The Hero Twins also appear in a Zuni story, which features a man-eating giant known as the Swallower of Clouds. The giant is so-called because he squeezes the clouds into his mouth for drink. Because of his mighty thirst, there are no clouds and therefore no rain. The crops wither and die, and the people are hungry. To the Indians of the Southwest, few things are more important than rain and the clouds are therefore seen to be powerful and benevolent. In order for the rain to return, therefore, the Hero Twins seek out the Swallower of Clouds to destroy him. They have to ask for the help of Grandmother Spider to achieve their task.

The katchinas arrive at the Hopi villages in the New Year for the Powamu corn ceremonies. These two have brought sprouted corn from the kiva to be distributed among the people.

CUSTOMS AND BELIEFS

There are over 250 katchinas in the Hopi religion. Katchinas live in mountains, springs and lakes. During the year they leave their homes and visit the villages to perform their dances. In the past the katchinas were believed to dance in their own forms. Today they are represented by the masked dancers who come out of the kivas. This carved wooden katchina figure represents a lightning katchina.

A Navajo priest treats a sick child. Illness is seen as a breakdown in the harmony and balance of the Universe. In a healing ceremony, the priest sings sacred songs, and uses special items like prayer sticks or a gourd rattle. All healing ceremonies are carried out in a strict order and must be word perfect. If the priest makes a mistake, evil may result. If the healing ceremony is successful, it is considered a guarantee of health and well-being for all the Navajo people.

For all Indians, religion was an essential part of their everyday life. Although some peoples of the Southwest have become Christians, many retain the beliefs and customs of their ancestors. It was the custom of the original Indians of the region to aim to live in harmony with the universe. They believed that if they co-operated with nature, it would give them rain, good crops and everything else that they needed.

A CYCLE OF CEREMONIES

Observing the annual cycle of religious ceremonies occupied much of the peoples' time. The rites associated with winter began in mid-July, at the time of summer rains and harvest. Ceremonies were held in the kivas, where members of the societies fasted, prepared altars and made offerings of feathered prayer sticks. These continued through to the winter solstice in mid-December. A new fire was then made to mark the beginning of summer – the time of the katchinas.

THE SACRED KATCHINAS

Many tribes, like the Hopi, believed that animals and plants had spirits which they called katchinas. They had many dances and ceremonies through which they would tell the story of the creation of the world, and summon the katchinas to help them in their lives.

Katchina spirits were believed to be invisible. At ceremonies, therefore, men from different clans dressed in special costumes and wore masks over their heads to represent the katchinas. The men believed that when they did this, and performed the right dances, the katchinas entered into them, and could be persuaded to use their powers to help the people.

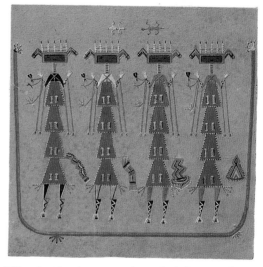

When the 'chant' was over, the sandpainting was always destroyed. However, some artists paint designs on board, like this one, for sale to tourists.

INITIATION

Men imitated both male and female katchinas, since it was only the boys who were initiated into their mysteries. Between the ages of five and nine, Pueblan boys were brought into the kiva for the first time, where they were confronted by masked 'scare katchinas' who whipped them to drive the badness out of them. Then, when they were between 11 and 14 years old, the boys made a second visit and received a second whipping. After this the katchinas removed their masks and revealed that they were really priests.

DIRE PUNISHMENTS

The priests explained that they became katchinas when they wore the masks. The boys were threatened with dire punishment if they failed to keep this secret, and then underwent a long training in the duties of the kiva society. Once they were married, they were ready to impersonate the katchinas themselves.

SINGS

The Navajo had many ceremonies that were devoted to the cure of illness, since they were frightened of sickness and death. All chants, or 'sings' as they were called, were curing ceremonies. The sacred songs were told or sung by the singer over the patient in a ceremonial hogan.

This figure is from a kiva mural at Kuana pueblo. It dates from about 1500. Kuana pueblo was abandoned after the Spanish invasion.

**'In the chief's kiva
They, the fathers,
They and Muyinga
Plant the double corn-ear
Plant the perfect double corn-ear
So the fields shall shine
with tassles white of perfect
corn-ears.'**

——— *Hopi corn ceremony* ———

SANDPAINTING

When a person was ill, their family sent for a singer. He would gather special herbs, pollen and coloured sands to be used for 'dry paintings' which were part of a healing ceremony. The singer brought these items into the hogan, sang the chants and made the paintings on the floor by sifting the multi-coloured sand through his thumb and forefinger to produce beautiful, delicate symbolic designs. The 'sing' went on for up to four days. At the end of the ceremony, the sick person sat in the middle of the final painting and the sand was stuck onto their body, bit by bit.

39

The large kiva below is based on Anasazi ruins found in New Mexico. The kiva was surrounded by a huge pueblo with about 500 rooms. At some stage, the great kiva shown below also had doors in the walls at ground level, giving access to the rooms surrounding the main chamber. These doors were later sealed up.

Some Pueblo Indians met in rectangular kivas, such as the Hopi kiva shown when the see-through page is turned.

Kivas were the religious centres of the Pueblo Indians. These were secret underground chambers, built by ceremonial societies and clan groups for use in religious rites or as meeting places for the men.

KIVAS

Kivas were usually circular in shape. The earliest examples, like those in Chaco Canyon, resembled huge, round drums. They were often constructed in the plaza, although after the Spanish conquest and attempts to impose Christianity on the natives, kivas were hidden from view in the dwelling blocks.

UNDERGROUND

The kiva was built at least half underground, like a semi-basement dug deep into the rock of the mesa. It had a flat roof, supported by log beams and covered with adobe. People entered the chamber through a smoke hole in the roof, using stout wooden ladders, some of them up to 10 metres long.

1 **Stone walls**
2 **Rooms surrounding kiva**
3 **Doorway to outer room**
4 **Wall ladder from kiva to surrounding room**
5 **Pillars supporting roof**

SACRED OBJECTS

Inside the kivas, clan members and priests kept their sacred objects, including prayer sticks, painted feathered masks and their costumes for the katchina dances.

In the middle of the kiva floor was a shallow stone-lined pit, symbolizing the 'sipapu'. The sipapu was believed to be a place of great mystery and spiritual power in the far north, where it was believed that humans had first entered the world from underground. Lining the walls were ledges used as benches for participants and spectators at ceremonies.

6 **Roof of poles, splints and earth**
7 **Possible smoke hole or entrance**
8 **Mud-plastered wall**
9 **Mural**
10 **Firebox in kiva floor**
11 **Altar**

DECORATION

The walls themselves were decorated with large paintings of Indian symbols in rich colours. These murals were not purely decorations: they actually formed part of the sacred ceremonies performed in the kiva. In fact, when the chamber was not being used for a religious function, the murals were covered with a layer of plain plaster to prevent them being seen by unauthorized people.

A MEETING PLACE

The kiva was used for activities besides ceremonies. It was the meeting place for a pueblo's governing council and the priests. It also traditionally housed a loom, on which the men wove their ceremonial sashes, and some kivas may have been used for social occasions. Kivas were named after the societies that met in them, such as turquoise, squash and fire kivas.

For ceremonial purposes, most kivas could be entered through an opening in the roof. Turn over the see-through page to see a diagram of a six-directions altar used in Hopi ceremonies. The six directions are north, south, east, west, up and down.

During the mid-19th century, the Indians of the Southwest met a new people – the white Americans. European settlements on the East Coast of North America had been established for 300 years, and settlers were now travelling westwards, seeking land and gold.

THE MEXICAN-AMERICAN WAR

Spanish rule in the Southwest had been replaced by Mexican rule after the 1821 War of Independence. Only 25 years later, the area was again caught up in war, this time against the land-hungry United States. Fighting ended in 1848 with the Treaty of Guadalupe Hidalgo, which ceded the territories of California and New Mexico to the United States.

THE PUEBLO REVOLT 1848

Many of the Indian peoples in New Mexico were opposed to American rule. Some plotted to recover New Mexico for the Mexicans. In 1848, a group of Mexicans and Pueblo Indians joined forces and killed the newly-appointed American governor, Charles Bent. Retaliation was swift. The US Army marched in, massacring many Indians, and eventually forced them to surrender.

SETTLERS

As a result of the change of rule, a flood of white American settlers now moved into the area. Many Indians saw their culture and traditional way of life threatened. The Navajo, who had previously raided both the Spanish and the Mexicans, now turned on the white settlers. The settlers appealed for help, bringing the Navajo into direct confrontation with the US government.

The 'gold rush' of 1848-49 resulted in thousands of prospectors flocking across Apache land to seek their fortune. Most of these men had little sympathy or understanding for the Indian peoples, and clashes inevitably followed.

THE NAVAJO WARS

The American government was already fighting a civil war with the Confederate states. Therefore it decided to subdue or destroy the entire Navajo people, and ordered Colonel Kit Carson and his soldiers to restore order.

Troops hunted down and killed the Navajo wherever they could find them. They also butchered the sheep, cattle and horses, burned the hogans and destroyed crops, smashing the Navajo economy and starving the people into submission.

THE LONG WALK

Some Navajos escaped into the mountains, but about 8,500 were forced to march to Fort Sumner in the Bosque Redondo, New Mexico. It was a journey of hardship and terror. The 500-kilometre trip was made on foot – it is still spoken of as the 'Long Walk'. People were shot down on the spot if they complained about being tired or ill, or if they stopped to help someone. Worse conditions awaited them at Bosque Redondo, which was like a death camp. Hundreds died of hunger or bad water.

The Navajo were held at Bosque Redondo for four years, until they signed a peace treaty with the government. They pledged themselves to peace with the white man in return for reservation land, sited on part of their traditional lands. Thus they returned to the Southwest, where they attempted to resume their way of life.

'I was living quietly and contented, doing and thinking no harm... I was behaving well. I hadn't killed a horse or man, American or Indian. I don't know what was the matter with the people in charge of us. They knew this to be so, and yet they said I was a bad man and the worst man there, but what harm had I done?'

— *Geronimo* —

THE APACHE

Meanwhile, the fierce Apache were defending their lands, using hit-and-run tactics. The leader of one group, Chief Cochise, fought off the US Army for 10 years. It was not until 1873 that he and his followers were rounded up and marched to the San Carlos reservation.

Another Apache leader, Geronimo, held out longer. However, he too was finally forced to surrender. In 1886, the last free Apaches were imprisoned in Fort Marion, Florida. From there, they were sent to Oklahoma, where Geronimo died in 1909.

Navajo chiefs such as Manuelito and Barboncito led thousands of the Dineh into Canyon de Chelly to avoid capture by the US Army. But they were hunted down and massacred by Kit Carson and his troops.

Geronimo, aged about 56. By the time this picture was taken in the 1880s, he had become the most famous and feared of the Apache leaders.

43

The Indians' attitude towards land shows how their beliefs were quite different from the white settlers. The Indians believed that land could not be owned by people, but was looked after by the gods and spirits for the use and benefit of all. If the land was treated badly, it would die. In contrast, the attitude of most of the European and American settlers was that all land could be bought, owned and used however a purchaser chose.

THE RESERVATIONS

By the end of the 19th century, the Indian peoples of the Southwest had been driven from most of their traditional lands by the whites. They had been forced onto land 'reserved' for them, called reservations. This land was usually of inferior quality: the soil was poor and there were only a few plants for the animals to eat.

Like their neighbours on the Plains, the peoples of the Southwest were encouraged to adopt the way of life and culture of the whites. However, the Indians reacted as they always did, by clinging fiercely to their own religions, languages, traditions and homelands.

The beautiful terrain of Monument Valley is in the part of Arizona known as the Painted Desert. This area forms part of the Navajo Reservation.

THE STRUGGLE FOR THE LAND

Then, at the beginning of the 20th century, it was discovered that reservation land was not so useless after all. The US government began to make attempts to take land back, away from the reservation Indians. In the 1900s the US Forestry Service took over the mountains and Blue Lake near Taos pueblo – land that was sacred to the Pueblo Indians. The Service promised the Indians that they could still continue their religious rites and practices on the land without interference. It was a promise that they did not keep.

The Indians then began a 40-year-long struggle to try to get the stolen land back. They took court actions and made many journeys to Washington to plead their case, but were blocked by white interests. Victory did come, though, in 1968, when President Richard Nixon signed a bill returning the stolen territory.

OTHER STRUGGLES

Elsewhere in the Southwest, a dam was built on the Colorado river at Glen Canyon, flooding part of the Navajo reservation. Oil, coal, uranium and other minerals were discovered in the area, bringing a new kind of intruder into Indian country – coal companies and multi-national corporations intent on mining the 'black gold'.

Juan Hubell's trading post in the late 19th century, when Navajo weaving had become a true commercial enterprise. Hubell hung watercolour paintings of his favourite designs on the walls of the trading post as models for Navajo weavers.

Indians love to get together to perform dances and exchange stories, at inter-tribal gatherings called 'powwows'. This one is the annual meeting at Taos pueblo.

INTER-TRIBAL DISPUTES

One of these areas had been the scene of a long-standing dispute between the Navajo and Hopi. In the 1880s, after boundary changes by the federal government, the Navajo moved into Hopi territory and set up sheep farms, restricting the Hopi to a small part of their original reservation. The dispute continues to this day.

Today, the Navajo are the largest Indian group in the United States – they number approximately 140,000. Most of these live on a reservation covering parts of Arizona, New Mexico. The area is sometimes called the 'Painted Desert' because the earth, stones and cliffs are bright red, or white, yellow and brown, and there are mounds of blue and grey clays and all kinds of minerals in the earth.

INDIANS TODAY

In spite of these great difficulties, Navajo, Hopi and other Pueblo Indians today continue to perform their dances and ceremonies, plant corn and herd sheep. Navajo women weave the sheep wool into rugs and blankets and sell them to tourists. Others make jewellery, pottery and baskets based on traditional designs. Thus the Southwest has managed to cling to tradition in the face of much hostility and hardship.

The ruins of the Anasazi settlement of White House, situated close to a river, are dwarfed by the cliffs of the Canyon de Chelly. It is not surprising that tourists want to visit the American Southwest, for this is some of the most beautiful country in the world.

As coal companies expand their operations onto Navajo land, pollution spreads, and the farmers are forced to travel long distances to find suitable grazing for their sheep. Many Indians are fighting to stop this kind of environmental destruction.

KEY DATES AND GLOSSARY

This book describes the history and way of life of the desert peoples of the Southwestern USA. Despite the influence of the Mexicans, Spanish and eastern American settlers, many of them live according to their traditional ways.

c15,000 BC Paleo-Indians cross from Asia into North America and spread across the continent.

AD 200-1300 The Anasazi (Basketmaker and early Pueblo cultures) populate the southwest region.

1492 Christopher Columbus comes across America, and mistakes it for Asia.

1541 Spaniard Francisco Coronado tours the Southwest and makes contact with the Indians of the pueblos.

1598 Juan de Onate founds the first Spanish colony in the Southwest.

1629-33 The first Christian missions are established by the Spanish among the Hopi, Acoma and Zuni tribes.

1680 Po-pe leads a revolt of the pueblos against Spanish rule.

1848 The Treaty of Guadalupe Hidalgo is signed by the USA and Mexico, ceding the area to the USA.

1864 The 'Long Walk' of the Navajo.

1868 The Navajo Reservation is created.

1886 Apache chief Geronimo surrenders, bringing Indian warfare in the USA to a virtual end.

1922 The Pueblo Indians unite, forming the All Pueblo Council to protect their lands against encroachment.

1924 US citizenship is granted to all Indians.

1962 The US government establishes a 'Joint Use Area' on Indian land, worsening the Navajo-Hopi dispute.

1968 Return of Blue Lake to Taos pueblo.

1982 The Joint Use Area is divided between the Navajo and Hopi, forcing resettlement on members of both tribes.

The name Hopi means 'the peaceful ones'. These people have lived in their traditional villages on top of three mesas for more than a thousand years.

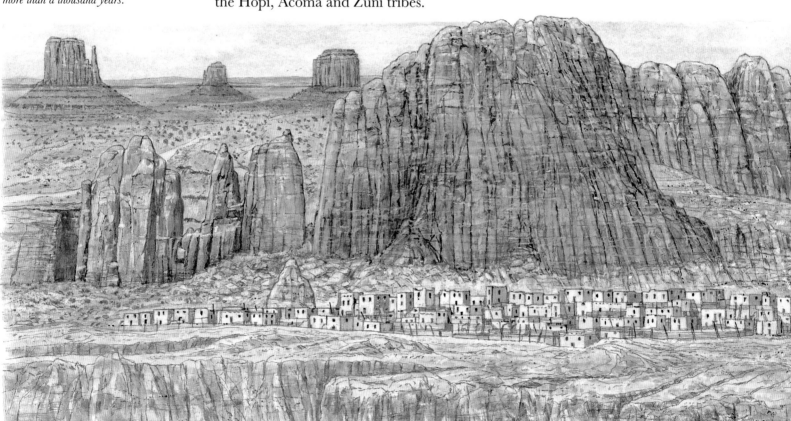

Glossary

adobe: sun-dried bricks, used by the Pueblo Indians to build their homes.

Anasazi: the name comes from a Navajo word meaning 'The Ancient Ones'. Their history and culture is subdivided into the following periods of development: Basketmaker (AD 200-700); Pueblo 1 and Pueblo 2 (AD 700-1050); and Pueblo 3 (AD 1050-1300). The modern Pueblo Indians are descended from the Anasazi.

Apache: a nomadic peoples, named from a Zuni word meaning 'the enemy'. They call themselves the 'Tineh' or 'The People'.

Dineh: Navajo word meaning 'The People'.

Hohokam: an early farming people.

Hopi: the short form of 'Hopitu', 'the peaceful ones', the name used for themselves by the peoples of northeast Arizona.

katchinas: spirit people, or dancers representing the spirit people.

mesa: a high steep-sided plateau or table-land, characteristic of the Southwest.

Mogollon: ancient peoples of southern Arizona and New Mexico.

Papago: a nomadic people of southern Arizona, also known as the 'People of the Desert'.

Pima: People of southern Arizona who call themselves 'O-o-dam', meaning 'The People'.

sipapu: the hole through which native peoples emerged from one world to another. Every kiva has one in its floor.

sweat lodge: a ceremonial lodge in which steam baths like saunas are taken.

wickiup: traditional Apache dwelling made of brushwood.

Yuma: farming peoples inhabiting the lower Colorado river.

Zuni: a pueblo people of New Mexico who call themselves 'Ashiwi', translated as 'the flesh'.

Quotations

Most of the quotations in this book are traditional songs or saying. They have been collected in *Mother Earth Father Sky* by Marcia Kegan, Wildwood House, 1974, and *Dancing Teepees* by Virginia Driving Hawk Sneve with Stephen Gammell, 1989. Geronimo's famous speech is quoted in *The Way: An Anthology of American Indian Literature*, Shirley Hill Witt and Stan Steiner, Vintage Books 1972, and the words of the Pueblo elder in *Handbook of the North American Indians vol 9*, Smithsonian Institution 1979.

INDEX

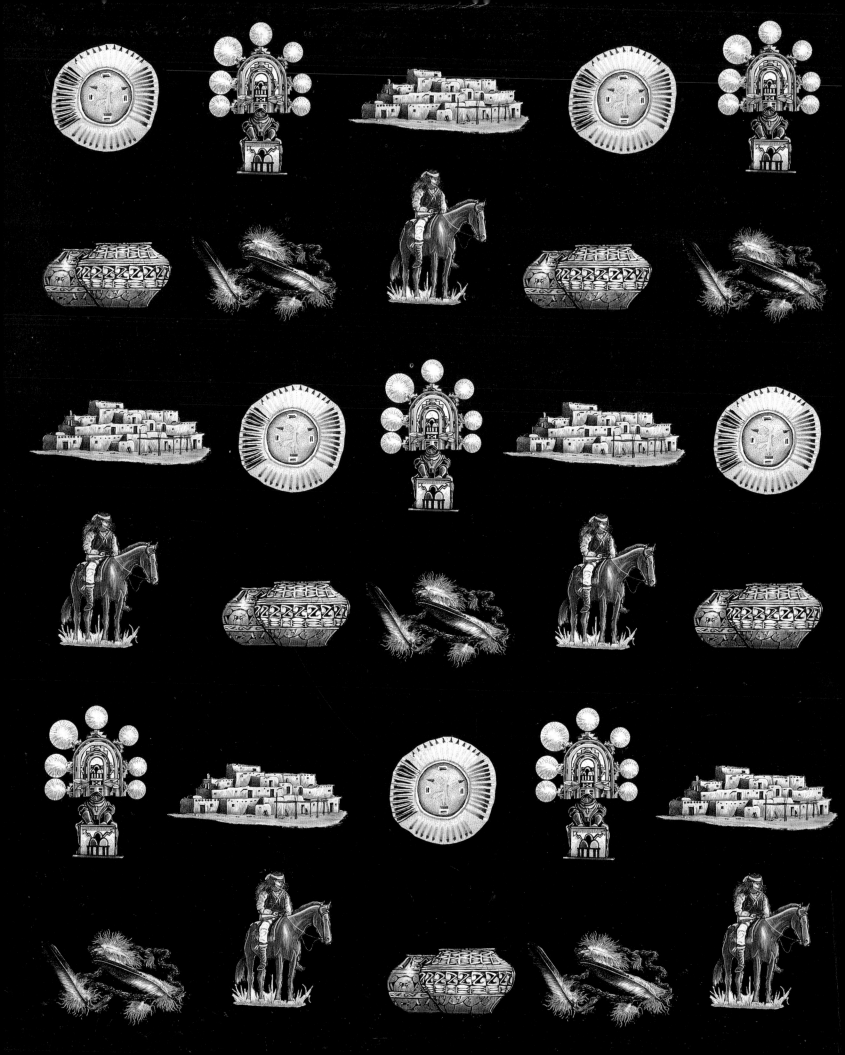